SPETSES

today and yesterday

ΕΚΔΟΣΕΙΣ
ΤΕΧΝΗ
EDITIONS

ATHENS 2004

© Copyright 2004   MICHAEL TOUBIS PUBLICATIONS S.A.
Nisiza Karela, Koropi, Attiki.
Telephone: +30 210 6029974, Fax: +30 210 6646856
Web Site: http://www.toubis.gr

ISBN: 960-540-457-5

CONTENTS

The beach at Vrellos.

The islands of the Argolic and Saronic Gulfs
are priceless jewels, gracing both gulfs
with their bountiful beauty.
The Athenians are lucky that they can reach
these islands in such a short time,
far from the noisy city.
At the entrance of the Argolic Gulf is Spetses,
picturesque and green. With a long nautical
tradition, its fleet and brilliant sailors played
an important role in the Greek War
of Independence against the Turks.
The luscious-green island of Spetses
is three hours by boat from Piraeus.
If the journey were to be undertaken by hydrofoil,
which services all these islands (except Salamis),
then the journey time would be reduced to about a third.
Spetses provide an opportunity for a brief escape.

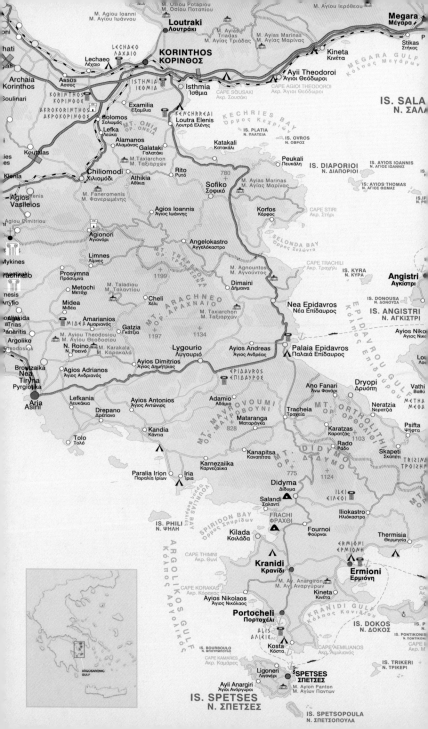

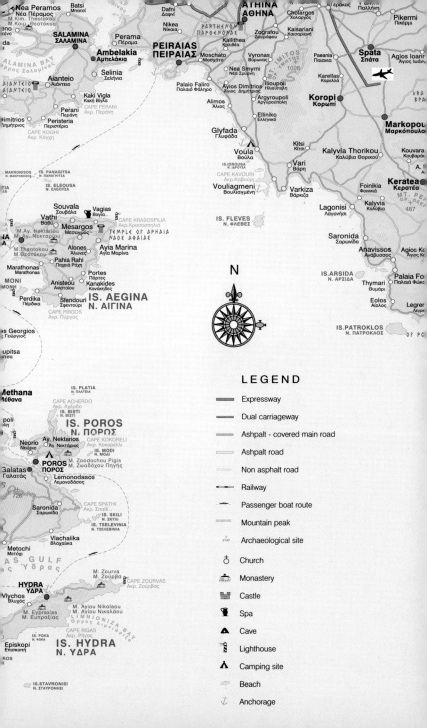

Spetses

The island of Bouboulina

*T*his island at the entrance of the Argosaronic has its own charms. There are no bare mountains. Instead, Spetses has green hills which slope gently down towards the sea. The horizon is open, and the colours of the light shine unimpeded, filling the place with life. The town of Spetses spreads out lazily along the length of the beach, only rising gradually in the centre, towards Kastelli, where the first inhabitants of the island chose to settle. Below Kastelli is the famous port of Dapias, with the raised beach and the cannons which protected the island from attack by the Turks during the Revolution of 1821. Behind Dapias are some of the town's finest mansions and below, just off the centre of a giant square to the right, proudly stands the bronze statue of the heroine Bouboulina, who gave her all to the Struggle of 1821. Bouboulina was the legendary female captain, who started off with her ships from the island to besiege Nafplion and Monemvasia. After this, charging along on a white horse, she was the first to enter Tripolitsa as it was being freed from the Turkish yoke.

To the south of Dapias is the pretty Palio Limani, the Old Port, with the old shipyards. Here some Spetsiots still continue the ancient craft of wood carving, and the Old Port adds its own touch to the town of Spetses. The town is, without a doubt, the main point of attraction for visitors. Yet, the town has one more great advantage: its wonderful beaches. The spacious Ayii Anargyri and the wonderful Ayia Paraskevi on the south coast, with Zogeria and Vrellos, where the sea takes on amazing colours, on the north coast. This combination, along with

Painting of Bouboulina from the Museum of Spetses.

LEGEND

	Ashpalt-covered main road
	Surfaced road
	Non-surfaced road
🍶	Archaeological site
⚲	Church
⛪	Monastery
🏰	Castle
🏺	Spa
▲	Cave
🗼	Lighthouse
🗡	Camp site
⛱	Beach
⚓	Anchorage

⚓ **SPETSES**
ΣΠΕΤΣΕΣ

Ayios Mamas
Άγιος Μάμας

CAPE FANARI
Ακρ. Φανάρι ⚓

🗼 **M. Ayiou Nikolaou**
Μ. Αγίου Νικολάου

OLD
HARBOUR

✝
via
ada

✝ **Ayios**
Ioannis

Agia Marina
Αγία Μαρίνα ○

✝ **Ayia Marina**

AYIAS MARINAS BAY
Όρμος Αγίας Μαρίνας

Tris
artires

⛪ **M. Ayion**
Panton
Μ. Αγίων
Πάντων

ALAHNON BAY
Όρμος Αλαχνών

πενα
tena

KOUZOUNOU BAY
Όρμος Κουζουνού

ΟΠΟΥΛΑΣ - SPETSOPOULAS STRAIT

Ayios
Nikolaos
✝

N

CAPE SIKIA
Ακρ.Συκιά

ΟΡ. ΡΟΥΜΑΝΗ ΡΑΧΗ
MT. ROUMANI RAHI

IS. MIKRO
Ν. ΜΙΚΡΟ

IS. AGIOS IOANNIS
Ν. ΑΓΙΟΣ ΙΩΑΝΝΗΣ

Ayios
Ioannis
✝

S. SPETSOPOULA
Ν. ΣΠΕΤΣΟΠΟΥΛΑ

CAPE MAVROVRAHOU
Ακρ. Μαυροβράχου

CAPE METZO
Ακο. Μέτζο

the excellent tourist facilities, have made Spetses so beloved, that the island is deluged with tourists in the summer.

Geography   Spetses lies to the right of the entrance of the Argosaronic Gulf, and only 1.5 nautical miles from the Peloponnesian coast. The island is oval-shaped, with a surface area of 22 square kilometres, and a population of almost 4000, most of which lives in the town of Spetses. The island is 52 nautical miles from the port of Piraeus, with which there are daily connections. To the south-east of Spetses, and

very close by, is the luscious-green private island of Spetsopoula.

The island is covered in dense pine forest, with **Morphology** relatively low hills, the tallest of which is Profitis Ilias (252 metres) in the centre of the island. The coastline is full of large and small bays, the principal ones being Ayia Marina in the east of the island, Xylokeriza, the large bay of the Ayii Anargyri with the organised beach and summer houses, Ayia Paraskevi (these are all on the south and south-west coast) and Zogeria and Vrellos on the island's north coast.

Introduction

Map of Spetses by an unknown artist, engraving, 15 x 18.5 cm., 1584.

1, 2. Neolithic finds from the Museum of Spetses.

Ωn ancient times the island was known as Pityousa, i.e. pine-tree island. The island was inhabited in the Early Bronze Age (3rd millennium BC), as we can see from the finds at Ayia Marina. Older finds have been located in the region of Zogeria, such as a stone tool from the Mesolithic period and Neolithic arrow heads, all of which are now in the collection of the Museum of Spetses. Even so, it appears that the sites at which these artefacts

were found were not permanent settlements in these periods, and so these artefacts were possibly left by visitors from the neighbouring Peloponnese.

There is very little evidence for the periods which followed. From this we can conclude that the island had few occupants and that it was dependent upon the neighbouring cities of the Peloponnese. On the other hand, there are finds that prove that the island was inhabited during the later Roman and Byzantine periods, just as it is also known that the Venetians took over the island in 1204, calling it the Isola di Spezzie, i.e. the aromatic island. It is possible that today's name of Spetses, or Spetsai, derives from this, but the most generally accepted opinion is that it comes from "pitys", i.e. pine.

The Turks conquered the Peloponnese in 1460. A few years later the first Arvanites, Orthodox Christians of Albanian descent, began to arrive on the island. They were refugees attempting to escape Turkish persecution. The Arvanites were soon followed by Greeks from the Argolid, Hermione, Kynouria and Laconia, who were fleeing for the same reason. They lived together peacefully. Their common goal was to survive in a place that was free,

Icons from the Museum.

far from the dynasts. The greatest danger they now had to face was the pirates. They gathered together, then, on a hill, at a point which could not be seen from the sea, and built Kastelli there, on the ruins of a much earlier settlement.

In the beginning they rose livestock. Soon, however, they realised that the sea could offer them much more. Indeed, this was something that their neighbours on Hydra had already understood. So, they turned to fishing, something for which they needed ships. And in this too they were lucky, as their island was rich in pine trees, providing them with the raw materials with which to build their fishing boats.

The beginning was made with small boats, and they later progressed to building much larger ones.

The first hall of Spetses' Museum with the wooden ship figures and the entrance of the Museum eith the bust of Xatziyannis Mexis.

By the middle of the 18th century, then, Spetses had the second-largest fleet in the whole of Greece, after Hydra. With this fleet the Spetsiots, along with the Hydraiots, were able to control commercial shipping not only in the Greek seas, but throughout the whole Mediterranean.

In 1768, war broke out between Russia and the Ottoman Empire. The Russians sent Orloff to the Peloponnese in an effort to inspire a Greek uprising against the Turks. The events which took place in Greece at that time are today known as the 'Orlofika,' having taken their name from this Russian noble. In 1770, the Spetsiots came out on the side of the Russians, but the revolt failed and the Turkish reprisals were harsh. Kastelli was set alight and its inhabitants killed or imprisoned.

ΛΕΚΑΣ ΜΑΤΡΟΖΟΣ

1. Bust of Matrozos Lekas.
2. The Monument of Spetses' Sailor.

In 1794, the war between Russia and the Turks ended with the defeat of the Turks and the signing of the Treaty of Kutchuk Kaynarca. The Spetsiots were amnestied, they returned to their island and began to extend their town from Kastelli towards the coast. The Turks were obliged to open the straits of the Bosphorus, thus enabling free passage to the Black Sea. The Spetsiot captains took advantage of this, and, with Russian favour, now sailed towards the Black Sea. They shipped mainly wheat, not only to the whole of the Mediterranean, but even to the Baltic countries and America. The wealth began to flow through to the island, and was to increase even more later as a result of further developments.

The French Revolution broke out in 1789, and later the war between Britain and Napoleon. The British blocked the Mediterranean, but the only people who were brave enough to break through this blockade were the Hydraiots and the Spetsiots. Control of shipping was now in their hands. (We should note that the Spetsiots took part in all the uprisings of the Struggle for Independence, the most important being the uprising of Lambros Katsonis in 1790). We are now at the beginning of the 19th century, and the idea of a Greek revolution has become rooted deeply in the hearts of the Greeks. The territory had been prepared by the 'Filiki Etairia,' the Friendly Society, a secret revolutionary organisation whose members numbered leading Greek figures, including many Spetsiots. On 3 April 1821, then, Spetses became the first island to join the Revolution. Its fleet included fifty large ships and twenty-five smaller ones, all equipped with powerful cannons. Among these ships were those of the heroine Laskarina Bouboulina, her largest ship the 'Agamemnon', in which she herself sailed, leading the Spetsiot fleet. The achievements of this fleet, which united with those of Hydra and Psara under the command of Andreas Miaoulis, were so great that it would require a whole book in which to detail them. Here we shall refer to only the most important.

There were two garrisons in the Peloponnese that were in Turkish hands. These were at Monemvasia and Nafplion. Bouboulina was charged with blocking these off with her fleet. The blockade lasted for many years, but it was decisive and it was only because of Bouboulina's efforts that the two fortresses finally fell to the Greeks. Bouboulina did not just stick to the war at sea. Along with her brave, young men, she participated in the siege of the main town in the Peloponnese at the time, Tripoli.

All this happened in 1821, the year in which the War of Independence broke out. And the achievements of the Spetsiot fleet in the following years were as equally great. In 1822, it chased the Turkish fleet all the way to Souda in Crete; in 1824 it rushed to help the people of Kasos, Psara and Samos; in 1825 came the victorious battle at Kafereus.

2

1. The portrait and the relic of Bouboulina in Spetses' Museum. 2. The Greek flag and the flag of the revolution in between two canons at Faros.

ΜΗ ΕΓΓΙΖΕΤΕ

Also impressive were the occasions when the Turkish fleet was fired upon by Spetsiot fireships and of especial significance for the Spetsiots is the Naval Battle of Spetses, which took place on 8 September 1822 and the anniversary of which is celebrated on the island every year. The close of the War found the Spetsiots having used up all their wealth for the Revolution, and they were in very dire economic straits. The island kept up a little marine activity until the mid-19th century, when the final decline set in and the population of Spetses began to fall. A whole century needed to pass before the island could be brought back to life again with the development of tourism.

The sun drenches the town in beautiful colours with its last rays of the day.

Yesterday & today

*Spetsiots love
the sea and respect
traditions.*

People

The ancestors of the Spetsiots, the people who first settled on the island, were the Arvanites. The fact that Greeks also arrived a little after these first settlers does not really make much difference. The two people share the same fate. Both Arvanites and Greeks came from the Peloponnese to escape Turkish persecution. Their struggle from that point on was the same, to survive. We shall not distinguish between them. Both love freedom. They are rebellious, brave, adventurous, stubborn, honourable.

They demonstrated all these characteristics during the Ottoman period, and even more during the years of the Struggle for Liberation. As soon as the mayhem of the war passed and Greece was free thanks to their heroic efforts, they could then show another side to their character: their gentle and peaceful side, their sweet and calm side. The women helped greatly during the difficult years. They stood by their men during the Struggle, yet in the home they remained ideal home-makers and true noble women.

The Hydraiots have the same character more or less, yet both sets of islanders love the sea to such a great degree that it is difficult to say which of the two loves it more. This love of the sea is what first turned the Spetsiots to fishing, and later to shipping and trade. And it was this love that first made them wealthy and masters of the Mediterranean, allowing them to play such a leading role in the liberation of Greece. The Spetsiots know this for themselves, and are proud of the fact. They may have given their all to the Struggle, to have sacrificed their whole wealth for it, and to have come out of this victorious battle wretched and poor, but they did not regret what they did, and would certainly do the same again. The visitor can sense this from the moment that he steps foot on the island.

He can sense this national exhaltation everywhere. And here, just as in Hydra, he is welcomed by the cannons, lined up in a row beneath Dapias. In front of the Poseidonio, the luxury hotel built at the beginning of the 20th century, stands the bronze statue of Bouboulina, the island's heroine, the idol of the Spetsiots. The central square of the town, with its pebbled floor, has been named after the heroine, and there is a bust of her in its centre. All the public buildings fly two flags. One is the Greek flag and the other is the flag of the Revolution of 1821, with the cross and the slogan 'Eleftheria i Thanatos' (Freedom or Death). Over 170 years have passed since then, but the visitor who sees all these flags around him might wonder whether the war did not take place within the past decade. He steps into the one of the renovated mansions of the captains and sees the wealth which shipping had brought to the island. He proceeds towards the Old Port and is pleasantly surprised by the plethora of boats anchored there. Many of these are fishing boats. The Spetsiots may be more involved with tourism now, this is where most of their income comes from. But their old love for the sea has not disappeared. Their second source of income is shipping and fishing. Further down, the visitor will encounter the old keels and shipyards, there where in the 18th century the Spetsiots built their famous merchant vessels. Yet, he will be even more surprised when he sees that at four or five of these 'shipbuilders,' they are still building and repairing wooden ships.

1. Picturesque lane in the town of Spetses.
2. Even today one can find small dockyards in Spetses, which continue the centuries' old tradition.

2

Local cuisine

It would be a serious omission not to say a couple of words about the local cuisine. Most people believe that the island's only dish is fish 'a la Spetsiota'. The locals, however, tend to disagree and would suggest that the visitor tries some meat with quince, beef with chunky macaroni and Tsakonian (from Tsakonia in the Peloponnese opposite) myzithra cheese, and 'propyra' (first fire), a bread made of wheat which is similar to the traditional 'lagana' Easter bread, yet to which salt and pepper have been added. Moreover, the marzipans are delicius.

The local speciality, fish "a là spetsiota".

Customs

Just as the Spetsiots' love of the sea has not extinguished, neither has their dedication to their local customs. They might not have adhered to the traditions so much in recent years, but today there is a trend towards reviving these local customs. One of these is the wedding, which on Spetses, as in most parts of Greece, is an entire 'ritual' lasting for several days. It begins with the cleaning out of the house in which the couple is going to live, to which the bride's dowry is then brought. It is accompanied by musical instruments - violin and lute - which lead the procession. There follows the custom of the 'making of the bed,' when friends visit the couple and leave their gifts upon the bridal bed.

As might be expected, the wedding day itself is of the greatest interest. The bride is dressed in her home in the company of her friends, who sing as they take care of her. At the same time, the groom is being prepared in his own home. There is a special feature to this custom, the so-called 'barber's toast'. The barber, who has really to put his skills to the test in order to prepare the groom as best he can, is offered plenty of sweets and a very rich tip.

The ritual begins with the best man, who along with the 'violia' (the musical accompaniment of violin and lute), is the first to go and get the groom, along with the guests, in order to go to the house of the bride. A rug has been laid out at the front door of the house, and the groom must step on it to enter. At the entrance they are offered a spoon of 'pelte' (quince preserve). The groom takes the bride and, along with the local instruments which always lead the procession, they go to the church, singing a couplet known throughout almost the whole of Greece:

> Today there is a wedding
> in a beautiful orchard.
> Today the mother is to be separated
> from her daughter.

After the wedding ceremony, almond sweets, soumada (an almond drink), and svingos (home-made sweet fritters) are offered. The formal wedding reception takes place in the evening, where the splendid special breads known as 'petes' are offered. 'Petes' are made with various aromatic spices (cinnamon, cloves, orange peel, bay leaves) and decorated with little flags and various goodies. After the drinking and eating comes the dancing and song, to the accompaniment of local instruments.

In the old days, in addition to the violin and the lute there was also the santouri, a kind of dulcimer. With their music, these instruments gave the cue for the singing and dancing. The folk songs on Spetses come from the Aegean islands and the Peloponnese next door. There are very few locally-produced folk songs. We quote here from one of these pieces, which talks of a local spot on Spetses:

At Bouboulos'

wickers,
I kissed you,
but do not tell.

As for the dances, there are the island ballos (danced by couples) and the syrtos (a group dance), as well as the Peloponnesian Kala-matianos (a circle dance), which features over almost all of Greece, and many others. One can enjoy Spetsiot music and dance at the island's festivals. These had begun to die out, but today there is a movement for their revival. The main ones are: the festival of Ai-Yiorgis at Zogeria on 23 April, Zoodochos Pigi (after Easter) at the churches of Elonas, on 1 July at the Ayii Anargyri, the last Sunday of the Easter Carnival at Roloi Square, and on Clean Monday at Sourbouti and Kastelli. The anniversary of the naval battle of Spetses is celebrated on 8 September at the church of Panayia i Armata (Virgin Mary of the Fleet) with events lasting for several days, ending with a live reconstruction of the firing of the Turkish fleet and a fireworks display.

One might expect at these festivals to see the traditional Spet-siot costume being worn, but this only appears at the odd cultural event. And this is a pity, because the beauty of this dress competes only with that of Salamis, which is famed for its luxury and elegance.

Traditional men's costume from Spetses.

Cultural events

The Armata are perhaps the island's most important event, with a national and religious character, accompanied by many cultural events throughout the week, such as folk dancing, regattas, sporting contests, theatrical performances, photographic and art exhibitions, etc.

Tens of thousands of visitors (last year there were 60,000!) congregate on the small island each September in order to see the splendid reconstruction of the 1822 Spetses naval battle from close up in the central port. The events of the Armata reach their peak with the firing of a reconstruction of the Turkish flagship amid a fantastic firework and light display that floods the sky. Visitors can watch the spectacle from the docks or even take part in the 'battle' as members of the opposing fleets from within one of the boats that will be afloat.

Impressive reconstraction of the Spetses naval battle. (Ph. Lynn Daly).

The Bios Open is also an important event, a free-diving competition featuring attempts to break the world record at Spetses. The first efforts were made in 1998 by Danai Varveri, a student at the Physics Department of the University of Thessaloniki, who dived 35 metres below the surface without mask, fins or weights and who still holds the world record at "natural weight". Since then, visitors from all over the world have come to the island, as its deep waters are perfect for fans of freediving.

In 2004, the first freediving Olympic performance will take place at the Bios Open, in collaboration with the free-diving association AIDA (Association International for the Development of Apnea).

As for the arts and letters, we can start by mentioning the old historians Anargyros Hadjianargyrou and Anastasios K. Orlandos, the professor and member of the Athens Academy Georgios Sotiriou, the first great Greek female painter Eleni Altamourou-Boukouri, her son Yiannis Altamouras, also a painter, the poets Georgios Stratigis, Yiannis Pergialitis, Maria Botsi, Giorgos Logothetis and Kostas Kokrovic. We will end by mentioning the contemporary painters Byron Kesses, Voula Mathew-Kourouzi, Petros Argyris, the folk painter Nikos Mantas and the poet Captain Lefteris Marmatsouris, from whose poem 'Nostalgia' we quote here:

Arts and letters

Tonight I was nostalgic for you lady,
aristocrat, jewel of the Argolic,
and I came close to you in my mind,
feeling pain and joy,
on this distant journey of nostalgia.

We have already touched upon the architecture of the island in our discussion of the mansions of Bouboulina and Sotiris Anargyros in the town of Spetses. The former represents the old mansion style, with its simple design, external staircase of stone, the courtyard with the tall walls and also the interior with its wooden decor and rich furnishings. The latter mansion represents the newer buildings of the neo-classical style.

Architecture

the city

The town of Spetses is wonderfully charming. Its old three-storey houses with their simple design next to the sea are really impressive. Only here, there are no naked and precipitous mountains all around to give the town a grandiose air. The hills here are low and covered in vegetation, creating a calm and idyllic picture. Spetses welcomes its visitors at the historic **port of Dapias**. With its linear, raised pier, from the platform of which eight cannons lined in a row jut out. These are the same cannons that protected the town from the Turks during the Revolution of 1821. This picture intimates that here the memories of that period still remain fresh. Even if over 180 years have passed since then.

The boats moor a little past the entrance to the port, on the left. The 'sea taxis' are moored a little further up. This is what the speedboats which await their customers in order to transport them to the island's beautiful coasts and to those of the Peloponnese opposite are called. And, just as in Hydra, the little flag of the Revolution is a prerequisite on the sea taxis, placed alongside the Greek flag. These taxis, along with the horse-drawn carriages, are the only means of transport on the island, since cars are banned. From the piazza with the taxis onwards the road climbs up, soon reaching the raised section that we mentioned earlier. This is where most of the town's cafes are, jammed in together, with their

The historic port of Dapia with the beautiful mansions.

little tables on the pebbly road in front of the sea. A road that, for all its length and breadth, is laid with white and dark green pebbles which form different patterns. This kind of decoration, which requires much time and effort, is a centuries' old tradition on Spetses. We shall also see this pebbled flooring in the squares, courtyards and the pathways of the gardens of the mansions.

This road, which continues left and right from the port, is the town's main road. Full of shops, restaurants, pizza parlours and bars, it hustles and bustles, especially during the summer months.

1. The carriages are the only means of transport.
2. A sample of Spetses' neoclassic architecture.

Behind Dapias is Bouboulina Square, with its pebbled floor and the bust of Bouboulina, the island's heroine, in the centre. In the front of the square **the mansion of Sotiris Anargyros,** a leading entrepreneur in both Europe and A-

merica, stands proud. Anargyros amassed a great fortune and then returned to his homeland of Spetses, where he built many important buildings and became the island's great patron.

His mansion, a wonderful example of the neo-classical order, is a two-storey building with large verandas all around. The veranda on the upper floor was supported by columns which created a peristyle. A pebbled pathway with beautiful patterns and lined with palm trees leads, through the garden, to the entrance to the mansion.

The entrance of the mansion of Sotiris Anargyros and above a hall from the interior of the mansion.

The splendid **mansion** that belonged to **Laskarina Bouboulina** stands to the right of Sotiris Anargyros' mansion. The heroine of Spetses played an important role in the Struggle of 1821. Not just because she dedicated her entire wealth to building and arming war ships, but because she led the fleet herself, taking part in many battles. Among these were the sieges with her fleet of Nafplion and Monemvasia, which were occupied by the Turks, and the liberation of Tripolitsa. The Greek chieftains and her fellow fighters gave her the titles of Capetanissa (Lady Captain) and Great Lady.

After her death, Russia, under whose flag her merchant fleet sailed before the Revolution, bestowed upon her the honorary title of Admiral. Bouboulina, then, is the only women in the world to have received this title.

The entrance of the mansion of Laskarina Bouboulina and Halls from the interior (right).

In contrast to the mansion of Sotiris Anargyros, the mansion of Bouboulina is simple and in total harmony with the other old mansions, yet without lacking in grandeur. Today it operates as a museum, complete with a guided tour which is given in English and Greek. The visitor will have the chance

to see, amongst other things, the large wooden sitting room with its carved, wooden Florentine ceiling and the Florentine furniture, as well as the huge safe of the ship 'Agamemnon,' the flagship of its fleet, and the dining room with a beautiful icon of St Nicholas dating from 1811. Also on exhibition are Bouboulina's gun, with its carved handle, and her silk kerchief, embroidered with gold and silver.

Near the mansion of Bouboulina is another old mansion house, which once belonged to **Hadji-yiannis Mexis**, one of the island's leading notables during the great Struggle of 1821. This mansion was built between 1795 and 1798 with wings on both sides, and has a ground floor plus two further floors. Arched stoas in the building's facade lighten somewhat its heavy structure. Mexis' own private rooms were on the ground floor, whilst the women's and guests' rooms were on the first floor, and the 'great ontas' - room in Turkish - which was used as a function room by the family during the years of the Revolution was on the second floor. The Museum is today housed on the first floor, which has seven rooms.

1

ΧΑΤΖΗΓΙΑΝΝΗΣ
ΜΕΞΗΣ
1754 1844

Spetses' Museum
(Hatziyiannis Mexis' Mansion).
1. The bust of Hatziyiannis Mexis.
2. Items from the ceramic collection.
3. The hall with the wooden
ship figures.
4. The entrance of the Museum.

2

3

4

The first contains exhibits relating to the island's nautical tradition, including the wooden figure-heads from ships. The second room houses archaeological finds. Of especial interest are the so-called 'gravy trays,' spouted bottles from the proto-Helladic settlement at Ayia Marina. The third room is host to a collection of Byzantine and post-Byzantine icons. Two old maps are on display in the fourth room. The first is a map of Spetses that was published in 1896 and the other is a large map of Greece dating from 1884. The fifth room houses a collection of Eastern and European ceramics which had been brought to the island by Spetsiot sailors. Traditional costumes are on display in the sixth room. Amongst them stands out the bridal gown of the noble woman Anesto Lembesi. Finally, the seventh room houses the actual flag of the Revolution of 1821, sailors' weapons, portraits and the bones of Laskarina Bouboulina.

Spetses' Museum (Hatziyiannis Mexis' Mansion). 1. Costumes from the Museum. 2, 3. Views from the hall of byzantine art.

1

2

3

From Dapias to the Old Port (Baltiza)

From Dapias, the central road continues in a south-east direction, parallel with the coast. It soon arrives at a sandy beach, a little before the **church of Ayios Mamas**. This is the nearest beach where you can swim, and it attracts many people in the summer. This is also the bus stop from which the buses which run the few connections for the island's distant beaches leave.

A little beyond Ayios Mamas, higher up than the sea, is the elegant building of the **Capodistrian Cultural Centre of Spetses**, which was recently repaired and renovated. It is painted white, with grey doors and grey steps. There is plaster decoration and the roof contains two pediments, on both the front and back, giving it the air of an ancient temple.

The splendid **Monastery of Ayios Nikolaos** is about 300 metres from the Cultural Centre, with its tall belfry and giant pebbled forecourt. Its cathedral church, today the Metropolitan church of Spetses,

2

1. *The Monastery of Ayios Nikolaos.*
2. *The Capodistrian Cultural Centre of Spetses.*
3. *The road from the Old Port (Baltiza) to Dapias.*

was built in 1805. It is a cruciform-style church with a dome, and next to it is a smaller church dedicated to three Spetsiot martyrs. The Monastery, freshly painted and well-cared for, looks over the sea from high up.

3

The coastal road that goes to the **Old Port (Baltiza)** passes beneath Ayios Nikolaos. Here, in the small bay formed beneath the monastery and the tall mansions, there is a pretty beach with blue-green waters. It is small, with fine pebbles and sand, and a few rocks at the edges. Here, swimmers can enjoy not just the waters but also the wonderful landscape.

The road continues around Ayios Nikolaos at this point and, having made a turn of 180 degrees, comes to the entrance of the Old Port. At the same moment, a new world, strange and idyllic, makes its appearance. Long and narrow, the bay of the Old Port seems to be endless. Countless colourful boats are anchored around it, from small boats to caiques and yachts.

There are houses all around, large and small, with old mansions scattered in between them. A pier standing at the start of the bay juts out a little into the sea. This pier was built for two reasons: in order to protect the port from the waves, but mainly so that large vessels could be moored to it. It is located opposite the lighthouse, which stands at the opposite side of the port. The dry land in the centre of the port slopes upwards a little. The houses at this point are built on both sides of the port, leaving a space for a small copse next to the beach, where the **War Memorial** has been erected.

As the road continues towards the mouth of the port, the picture become even more enchanting. Tavernas and ouzo bars offering fresh fish and other goodies are now added to the scene. The horse-drawn carriages come and go, transporting visitors to the tavernas or the sights of the port. This is where most of the mansions are situated, built by local or even Italian craftsmen. Among them stand out those of Botasis, Goumas and Vamvas. From here, a road to the right leads to the **church the Analipsi** (Ascension of Christ) and the district of the same name. The coastal road, which has now reached the cove of the bay, gradually begins to turn towards the

The beach on the west of the old port.

opposite direction, to the side of the Faros, as the lighthouse is called.

The first shipyards, where they repair the wooden ships, now make their appearance. In one of these, a large boat has been pulled out onto the sands. Its hull rests upon the wooden keels and it is held upright by wooden posts placed into the ground at its sides. There is a hole in the side which needs to be sealed, the masts have to be positioned, and the boat needs painting. This red does not seem to be its final colour. Further down from the shipyards are the old naval dockyards, where the Spetsiots built their merchant fleet in which they

The manina in the Old Port.

sailed throughout the whole Mediterranean. The technique of ship building is ancient. Its roots lie not just in the days when the ancient Greeks built their famous triremes, but reach as far back as the Bronze Age.

There are four or five small dockyards in the Old Port today, which continue the centuries' old tradition. On a large part of the eastern side of the port, then, one can see some wooden ships, the great majority of which are old, pulled up onto the dry land to await their turn for repair or maintenance. It is doubtful whether you will be to see such a sight, with so many such ships, anywhere else in Greece.

The arched buildings on the Old Port.

The road now passes the naval dockyards and enters a small pine forest. A little church painted yellow with a courtyard all around it somewhere to the right, grabs our attention.

This is the **Panayia Armata**, the Virgin Mary of the Fleet, built as a reminder of the Greek fleet's victorious battle against the Turkish fleet in the straits between Spetses and the Argolid on 8 September 1822. It is also a reminder of how the Panayia also saved the Spetsiots on that day. The danger arose when the Turkish fleet suddenly turned towards

The walk of the Cannon Station in Faros with the statue of Kosmas Barbatsis, and across from it the city.

Spetses with the aim of landing there. There were only a few people on the island able to defend it, and their chances of withstanding the threat nil. It was then, as most Spetsiots believe, that the Panayia helped them to think of a truly clever solution.

They placed a large number red fesia (caps) on top of some bushes in the area of the lighthouse. The Turks were deceived and believed that there was a large army on the island ready to defend it, so they did not attempt to land.

This victory was also a redemption, and the Spetsiots celebrate its anniversary on 8 September each year - also the birthday of the Panayia - with much fanfare. There is a re-enactment of the naval battle in the evening, when a reconstruction of the Turkish flag ship is fired. The celebration ends with fireworks, which fill the sky. The firing of the Turkish command ship during this historic naval battle was the decisive factor in the Greek victory. The brave fighter who managed to approach the Turkish ship and to set fire to it was the Spetsiot Kosmas Barbatsis. His compatriots honour him as well, and have set up his bronze statue on the cannon station at Faros.

The church of Panayia Armata.

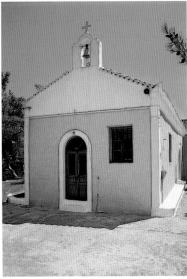

The lighthouse stands tall at the edge of the cape, in front of the entrance to the Old Port. The whole of this area has taken its name from the lighthouse, and is known as **Faros**, i.e. lighthouse in Greek. Next to the lighthouse are the installations of the military navy, and below this is the famous **Peripatos** (walk) along the cannon station. This is what they have called a park in front of the beach, about ten metres above the sea. The Peripatos is long and there are openings every four metres along its platform. These openings contain cannons, the same ones that protected the port during the Struggle of 1821. Behind the cannons, on top of a pile of stones, is the statue of Barbatsis. He holds a short staff in one hand and a torch in the other - the torch with which he set fire to the enemy's command ship. On the rise above the statue there stands a tall flagpole in between two cannons, with two flags at its peak: the Greek and once again, the Spetsiot flag of the Revolution, with the words 'Freedom or Death.' Both flags flutter in the light breeze, as though they wanted to tell us that the past is not so distant from the present. That the memories of what happened on this island, and in particular in the straits between Spetses and the Peloponnese, are still fresh for the Spetsiots.

A strange composition in metal on the sea below, representing a gorgon, catches our attention. It was made by the same artist who created the statue of Bouboulina.The walk in the park with the cannon station is very pleasant. One can sit for hours and enjoy the view of the Old Port, as seen from behind the cannons. If it is late in the afternoon, then one can remain here, in the little copse, until sunset. The sun will set behind the monastery of Ayios Nikolaos, adding a golden colour to the sea. And a glimpse of the gorgon can be caught, down on the beach, to the right.

The sunset at the lighthouse. on the right is visible the bronze statue of the mermaid.

*Faros with the Walk of the Cannon Station,
and across from it the city.*

Kastelli

Panayia
Daskalaki

Profitis Ilias

Behind Dapias, at a distance of 500 metres from the sea, is **Kastelli**, the oldest neighbourhood in the town. It is built high up, on the site of a natural fortress, with a wonderful view over the town of Spetses and the surrounding region. It is situated in between two streams, which protect it at the sides: the stream of Ayios Georgios to the left and that of Kounoupitsa to the right. It appears that the first inhabitants of the area chose this site on which to settle. The research which has been done shows that the first settlement dates to the classical period. Later, it was used as a refuge for people from Methana who had abandoned their houses after the

eruption of the Methana volcano in 273 BC. From that point on we have no other extant reference to the settlement, until the arrival of the Arvanites, Christian Orthodox of Albanian descent, in the middle of the 16th century. They came from the Peloponnesian coasts opposite, persecuted by the Turks, and many of them established a medieval settlement at Kastelli, on the site of the earlier settlement. By the beginning of the 17th century, then, Kastelli had evolved into a fully-developed settlement, with a fortification wall which it is said had seven gates. This settlement was the original core of the town which later expanded towards the sea.

Kastelli, the oldest neighbourhood in the town.

All this took place during the Turkish occupation of Greece. During the war between Russia and Turkey from 1768 to 1794, the Spetsiots took part on the side of the Russians and rose up against the Turks. As a punishment, the Turks raided Spetses in 1770 and set fire to Kastelli, killing or imprisoning its inhabitants. The destruction of Kastelli by the Turks completed the deterioration already caused by the passage of time. Today, only three of the churches survive in the old city, whilst the houses all

around are new. The first church which the visitor shall encounter whilst walking up the narrow neighbourhood lanes is that of the **Ayia Triada** (Holy Trinity, late 18th century), a three-aisled basilica with a dome and a wide belfry. Next comes the church of the **Taxiarches** (Archangels, early 19th century), a cruciform-style church with a dome and wall paintings. Both these churches are built in a simple style with thick walls. The third church is that of the **Koimisi tis Theotokou** (Dormition of the Virgin), a beautiful post-Byzantine cruciform-style church, with a dome and old wall pain-tings. This church is the oldest of the three, dating to the 17th century, and was the Metropolitan church of Spetses during the Revolution. The local chieftains swore their allegiance to the uprising in this church in 1822. Tradition mentions a miracle of the Panayia, the appearance of a giant spring with water, which saved the church from the fire that the Turks had set to it.

One can ascend directly to the wooded peaks of the island from Kastelli, although this is a little difficult as there is no specific footpath. The best solution is to follow the dirt road located close to the left, which eventually leads to the island's crest. This road, which is not really suitable for walking along, leads to the kiosk known as the 'hunters' meeting point'. A little further down is the **Panayia tou Daskalaki**, a little church built among the pine trees on the plateau formed at the peak of the mountain. The view from here over Kastelli, the rest of the island and the coasts of the Peloponnese opposite, is breathtaking. A little to the left is the peak of the Profitis Ilias, the island's highest.

1. The Koimisi tis Theotokou.
2. The Panayia tou Daskalaki.
3. The Taxiarches.
4. The Ayia Triada.

4

From Dapia to Kounoupitsa

Beneath the cannon station of Dapias, to the right as we enter the port, there is a great square in front of the sea. In the south-west corner of the square stands the luxury **Poseidonio hotel**, an architectural masterpiece of the early 20th century. With its large doors and windows, heavy iron railings around the balcony and columns at the entrance, it is one of the sights of Spetses most worth seeing. This hotel has hosted many important figures of the 20th century.

In the centre of the great square, which can be considered as the pier of the hotel, is the **bronze statue of Bouboulina**, the heroine of the island and idol of all the Spetsiots. She has one hand reaching for the handle of her gun, which is bound around her waist, and the other raised to her forehead a little above the eyes, as though trying to spy some enemy ship sailing in the distance.

The walk along the beach of **Kounoupitsa** after the Poseidonio hotel is most enjoyable. Most of the houses were built after the Struggle of 1821, and the town of Spetses has expanded at a fast pace along the length of the beach. The greatest growth has been noted after the middle of the 20th century, when many luxury hotels, shops, tavernas and bars have been built, making Kounoupitsa an attractive destination for tourists.

Thankfully, in spite of the economic flurry, some old mansions have been preserved in among the new houses. These include Bouboulina's summer house, the mansion of Boukouras, the Town Hall - the white building with the roofed, domed entrance and the pink oleander, which was initially also a residential mansion. The old Daskalakis textile factory is interesting, a rare example of industrial architecture. Today it hosts a luxury hotel.

The statue of Bouboulina.

Opposite page:
The Poseidonio hotel and views from Kounoupitsa.

After Kounoupitsa comes the village of **Sourbouti**, although the border between the two is not especially clear. Sourbouti can also be considered as the edge of Spetses town, and here the buildings begin to peter out. And yet, this last part of the town has many interesting features.

The fine complex of the **Anargyrios and Korgialenios School** is to be found here, another creation of Sotiris Anargyrou, which operated for almost 50 years from 1927. This school, something akin to today's colleges, was considered one of the best in Europe and for this reason counted many non-Greeks among its pupils. In front of the school is the pretty copse which separates it from yet another of the beautiful organised beaches. It is located at a spot where the sand is drawn out, forming a tongue within the sea.

There are other beaches at which you can take a swim along this walk from Dapias to Kounoupitsa. There is one in front of the first houses of Kounoupitsa, and another between Kounoupitsa and Sourbouti. But, the beach in front of the school is the best, and in terms of the natural surroundings as well, as it is far from the noisy town. From here, Dapias and Faros can only just be seen, like distance capes within the turquoise sea.

The beach in front of the Anargyrios and Korgialenios School.
Opposite page:
The beach of Kounoupitsa.

Tour of the

Spetses have a short coastline, without this meaning that these coasts lack any of the beauty of any other island. On the contrary, they hide the most idyllic beaches of the Argosaronic.

The tour of the island is done by 'sea taxi' (after an agreement with the owner of the boat), with caiques or rented motorcycles and bicycles. To stop off at one or more of the beaches (with the sea taxi) might be sort of expensive but what is important for the visitor is not just to glance at these wonderful

island (beaches)

beaches, but to stay for a while and to enjoy them this way. There is also another way in which to do this: to take the coach for, e.g., the beach of Ayii Anargyri at 11:00 or 12:30 in the morning and to return at 15:30 or 17:00 in the afternoon.

Our subject here, however, is the tour of the island, which will start from the port of Dapias in the direction of Faro. The visitor will have the opportunity at the beginning of this trip to see again some of the things he or she has already encountered. The old mansions in a row in front of the sea, the monastery of Ayios Nikolaos, the entrance to the Old Port. At Faros, the boat reaches very close to the lighthouse, turning at the cape. Just beyond this turn a little blue church set upon the rocks, in front of the sea, catches our attention. This is **Ayios Demitrios**.

The journey now makes its way along the island's eastern beaches. A little after Ayios Demitrios, the boat approaches **Ayia Marina**, an organised beach with pebbles and sand. The slopes of the mountain behind the sands are covered in pine and cypress trees. A pre-Helladic settlement over 3000 years-old has been discovered at Ayia Marina, the finds from which are now in the Museum of Spetses (see the Town of Spetses).

The journey continues initially towards the south and then towards the west. The luscious-green private island of Spetsopoula which belongs to the family of a shipowner (Niarchos) who has been a great benefactor to Spetses, can now be seen close by to the left.

1. The church of Ayios Demitrios.
2. The organised beach of Ayia Marina.

There are several villas built in among them, and at the peak of the hill stands the resplendent **convent of the Ayii Pantes** (All Saints), with a few nuns in residence.

The next organised beach is that of **Xylokeriza**. The thick pine forest that surrounded this little beach was burnt down a few years ago, and this has substantially reduced its charm. Today, only the beach's white sands and turquoise waters remain.

1. The convent of the Ayii Pantes.
2. The beach of Xylokeriza.
3. The largest and the most frequented beach of Ayii Anargyri.

Having covered almost half the tour of the island, the boat now turns towards the south-west, heading for the largest and most frequented beach on the island. This is the **Ayii Anargyri**, its beautiful sands spread out to form a large and open petal. There are thick pine trees all around it, among which many villas have been built. Ayii Anargyri is an organised beach with many water sports facilities and restaurants.

2

3

The beach of Ayii Anargyri.

At a short distance to the west of the beach is the **cave of Bekiris**, which acted as a refuge for the Spetsiots during the years of the Struggle against the Turks. The cave is located among some rocks before the sea, yet its entrance cannot be seen from the approaching craft.

On the next bay after the Ayii Anargyri is **Ayia Paraskevi**, the most delightful beach of Spetses. The bay at this point is very small and tighter than

The cave of Bekiris.

the previous one. The pine trees seem taller, more bushy at this bay, and there is not a villa in sight. The only building here is the brilliant-white **church of Ayia Paraskevi** on the south edge of the sands. Fortunately or unfortunately - this depends on your own personal preference - this beach is organised too. There are a few umbrellas and deck chairs, although fewer than those at Ayii Anargyri, and there is also a tavern.

The most delightful beach of Spetses, the Ayia Paraskevi, with its little church.

Our circumnavigation of the island continues. The boat proceeds as far as the cape which makes up the most westerly point of the island. Here, it changes direction and turns slowly towards the east. Another beach will soon make its appearance within this closed bay. This is **Zogeria**, with the brown sand and the thick pine trees all around. This is also an organised beach, with a restaurant hidden inside the forest. At the start of the beach there is a small set of stairs where passengers embark and disembark and where small boats are also tied. Here, one can observe something which is quite common at the pier of the Old Port. One of the island's many old cannons is set up upright with the mouth buried deep in the earth. It is secured so well that it is used as post to which the boats are tied. The cannon at the landing-place of Zogeria has been painted white, in contrast with those at the Old Port, which are completely black.

1, 2. Views from Ayia Paraskevi.
3. The cove of Zogeria, with the thich pine trees.

Traces of a pre-Helladic settlement such as that at Ayia Marina have been found at the cape, which is located at the end of the bay. Everything at Zogeria is very clean - the small landing-place, the sand, the restaurant - and the sea waters are crystal clear.

After Zogeria, the last beach that we will approach is the magical beach of **Vrellos**. The colours of the sea here are perhaps more beautiful than at any other of the island's beaches. The slope of the land makes the lively pine trees literally hang over the narrow pebbly strip. Theirs is a persistent and endless quest for food, irrespective of whether this is to be found over a calm or a stormy sea. After the beach Vrellos, one can visit

Ligoneri, the beach which is our final destination.

We have already begun our return to the starting point. A few scattered villages start to appear on the right of the boat, far from the town of Spetses. Now, the parts that the traveller has already encountered during his or her tour overland: the beautiful beach in front of the Anargyirios and Korgialenios School full of swimmers, Kounoupitsa, the old mansions, the Poseidonio hotel, and, finally, the port of Dapias with the cannon station.

Our tour of the island by boat finishes here, and along with it our tour of Spetses, the luscious-green island with the glorious history.

The beach of Vrellos.

ISLANDS A

Aegina

*Aegina has an area of 84 square kilometres
and is only 17.5 nautical miles from Piraeus Port.
It is an ideal place for short breaks away from Athens.
The churches with their glass domes,
the picturesque narrow alleys,
Angistri and the significant historical monuments
such as the Aphea Temple will win anyone over.*

UND SPETSES

Aegina

Things to see in the town and the port of Aegina
- The church of Ayios Nikolaos Thalassinos.
- The mansion of Voyiatzis.
- The traditional carriages.
- The mansion of Kanaris.
- The church of Panayitsa.
- The Folk Museum.
- The tower of Markellos.
- The house of Capodistrias.
- The Metropolitan church.
- The Monastery of Faneromenis.
- The church of Ayii Theodorii. (Beutiful Church).
- The archaeological site and the museum of Kolona.
- The Orphanage.
- The house of Kazantzakis.
- The Kapralos Museum.
- The tower of Zaimis.

Aegina

Things to see in the island of Aegina:
- The church of Ayios Nikolaos of Moulou.
- The beutiful settling of Kypseli.
- The village of Vathi.
- The settling of Souvala,
  the second port of Aegina.
- The monastery of Ayia Aikaterini.
- The little port of Vaia.
- The monastery of Ayios Nektarios.
- The hill of Palaiochora with the
  byzantine churches.
- The monastery of Chrysoleontissa.
- The Mesagros.
- The temple of Aphaia.
- The village of Pacheia Rachi.
- The ruins from the temple of Zeus Hellanios.
- The holly mountain Oros.
- The little island of Moni.
- The beaches of Ayia Marina and Portes.
- The tourist resort of Marathonas.
- The fishing village of Perdika.
- The organised beach of Aiginitissa.

Things to buy:
- Pistachios.
- Traditional ceramics.

Aegina

Angistri

Things to see in the island of Angistri:
- The church of Ayii Anargyri to the port at Skala.
- The little village of Metochi.
- Mylos, the biggest village of the island.
- The little port of Megalochori.
- The beach at Dragonara.
- Limenaria.
- The islet of Aponisos.
- The beach at Skliri.
- The beach of Halkiada.

Angistri

Salamis

*Salamis is the second largest of the Saronic
islands and the nearest to Athens.
It is covered in pine trees and has beautiful beaches,
especially on the south coast.
The island is best known for the historic
Battle of Salamis, which took place in 480 BC
between the victorious Athenians and the Persians.*

Salamis

Poros

Poros means passage,
and this is where the name of the island comes from,
since it lies in the south-east of the Saronic Gulf,
opposite the Argolid in the Peloponnese.
Located on the edge of this passage,
built on both sides of a hill, this island society
is a happy one.

Poros

Things to see in Poros:

- The mansion of Kanelopoulos.
- The Archaeological Museum.
- The traditional Roloi.
- The Metropolitan church.
- The mansion of Deimezis.
- The building of Progymnastiria.
- The Kanali.
- The «villa» Galini.
- The little harbour of Agapi.
- The islet of Daskalio.
- The sanctuary of Poseidon.
- The beaches at Askeli and Vagionia.
- The monastery of Zoodochos Pigi.
- The islet of Bourtzi.
- The beach of Mikro and Megalo Neorio.

Hydra

*Hydra is a wonderful, cosmopolitan society unto itself.
With its rich history, the island stands out for its charm
and the grand mansions of the captains
and notables of the 1821 War of Independence.
Cars are forbidden on Hydra, and transport
to the beaches is by caique only.*

Things to see in Hydra:
- The Historical Archive and Museum.
- Monastiri (Metropolitan church of Hydra).
- Periptero with the famous Spilia.
- The neighbourhood of Avlaki.
- The port at Kaminia.
- The mansion of Lazaros Kountouriotis.
- The traditional pharmacy of Rafalias.
- The Kala Pigadia.
- The monasteries of Ayios Nikolaos,
  Profitis Ilias and Ayia Evpraxia.
- The hill of Kaiafas.
- The coastal settlement at Vlychos.
- The beaches of Palamidas, Molos,
  Episkopi, Kaoumithi, Ayios Nikolaos.
- Nisiza and Limnioniza.
- Mandraki.

Hydra

Useful Information

For Spetses take the boat or ferry from Piraeus (information: Piraeus Port Authority tel. 210 4593123).

For a quicker journey, you can take the speedboat, again from Piraeus (from Akti Miaoulis or Zea). Information: Minoan Flying Dolphins, tel. 210 4199200 and Saronic Dolphins, τηλ.: 210 4224777.

You can even go to Spetses by car. Drive in the direction of Nea Epidaurus and then follow the new road for Koliaki, Kranidi and Kosta, which is opposite Spetses.

To get from Kosta to Spetses you must take the ferryboat (four connections a day from Kosta). You can also go by sea taxi at any time, day or night (tel. 22980 72072) or by the more traditional caique during the summer period. You must leave your car at Kosta, as on Spetses - as on Hydra - private cars are forbidden.

Cars are banned on Spetses, a detail that surely contributes to the felicity of the residents.

Specifically:

- cars are banned in the hamlet of Spetses,

- motorbikes and mopeds are banned from the centre of the Old Port from 17:30 until 02:00 from 1 June until 30 September.

Cars are not needed, and there are no car rental agencies. Bicycles and mopeds provide the perfect means for travel. You can rent them.

You can also choose a more traditional form of transport for getting about.

- **Traditional caiques:** you will find these in the central port, but there are no specific connections to the beaches - they leave once they are full. If you want to go to a beach with a group, the rental price depends upon the season as well as on your destination.

- **Traditional carriages:** you will find these at the port, tel. 22980 73171. Also, in front of the Poseidon Hotel, tel. 22980 73170. From 8:00 am until 1:00 am.
- **Speed boat taxis:** these are available all day and night at Spetses and Kosta: 22980 72072.
- **Buses:** there is a connection that goes over the whole island. There are 3-4 connections daily in high season.
- **Taxis:** you will find these at the port. There are four, which you can contact by mobile phone if they are not at the taxi rank in the port, tel. 6932 200240, 6944 605784, 6942 635656, 6944 605611.

Useful Telephone Numbers

Area code 22980
Spetses doctor's surgery 72472
Police 73100
Tourist Police 73744
Port authority 72245
Municipality 72225, 74517, 72588
Local development office 75211
Horse-drawn carriages 73171
Sea taxis 74885

The port of Dapia.

HOTELS

On Spetses there are many hotels and rented rooms, both in the town and in the other areas.

ECONOMOU			
MANSION	Kounoupitsa	Traditional Settlement	A
KASTRO	Spetses	Apartments	
LEFKA PALACE	Spetses	Hotel & Bungalows	A
NISSIA	Kounoupitsa	Traditional Settlement	A
TWIN HOUSE	Spetses	Pension	A
YACHTING CLUB INN	Spetses	Traditional Settlement	A
7 ISLANDS	Spetses	Hotel Apartments	C
8 ADELFIA THIMARA	Spetses	Studios	
AETHRIO	Spetses	Traditional Settlement	
ALEXANDRI	Spetses	Hotel	E
AMORE	Spetses	Studios & Apartments	
ANGELA	Spetses	Rooms to let	
ANNA - MARIA	Spetses	Hotel	E
ARGO	Spetses	Hotel	E
ARMATA	Spetses	Hotel	C
BI	Spetses	Pension	
CAMELIA	Spetses	Hotel	D
CHRYSSOULA	Spetses	Rooms to let	
CONDILLIA II	Kounoupitsa	Studios & Rooms	
DOUVROS	Spetses	Rooms to let	
FAROS	Spetses	Hotel	C
HORIZONTES	Spetses	Rooms to let	
ILIOS	Spetses	Hotel	C
KLIMIS	Spetses	Hotel	D
MAKIS - COSTAS	Spetses	Apartments	
MARGARITA	Spetses	Hotel	E
MIMOZA II	Spetses	Studios & Rooms	
MINA - TZENI	Spetses	Apartments	
NIRIIDES	Spetses	Studios & Apartments	
ORLOFF	Spetses	Apartments	
POSSIDONION	Spetses	Hotel	A
ROUMANI	Spetses	Hotel	B
SIRIOS	Spetses	Hotel Apartments	B
SOLEIL	Spetses	Hotel	C
SPETSES	Spetses	Hotel	A
STAR	Spetses	Hotel	C

STELIOS . . . . Spetses . . . . Hotel . . . . . . D
THEANO . . . . Spetses . . . . Rooms to let
TSAKALAKOS . . . . Spetses . . . . Rooms to let
VALIA . . . . Spetses . . . . . . Hotel Apartments C
VARLAMIS . . . . Spetses . . . . Apartments
VICTORIA . . . . Spetses . . . . Studios
VILLA ANESSIS . . . . Spetses . . . . Hotel C
VILLA ARETI . . . . Spetses . . . . . Studios & Rooms
VILLA ARGO . . . . Kounoupitsa . . . . Studios
VILLA CHRISTINA . . . . Spetses . . Traditional Settlement . . . . . . B
VILLA IRINI . . . . Spetses . . . . Xenonas
VILLA KALOMIRA . . . . Spetses . . . . Apartments
VILLA KRIEZI . . . . Spetses . . . . Rooms to let
VILLA MARINA . . . . Spetses . . . . Rooms to let
VILLA MARTHA . . . . Spetses . . . . Hotel C
VILLA MATA . . . . Spetses . . . . Rooms to let
VILLA METAXA . . . . Spetses . . . . Studios
VILLA MIMOZA . . . . Spetses . . . . Pension
VILLA MORIATI . . . . Spetses . . . . Rooms to let
VILLA ORIZONTES . . . . Spetses . . . . Rooms to let
VILLA PLAZA . . . . Spetses . . . . Pension
VILLA TONIA . . . . Spetses . . . . Apartments
VILLA ZAHOU . . . . Spetses . . . . Apartments

USEFUL WEBSITES:

http://www.greektourism.com/travel_guide/regions/attica/spetses
http://odysseas.gnto.gr/Map/map.html
http://www.spetses.gr/

INDEX

Texts: YIANNIS DESYPRIS
Text editor: DAPHNE CHRISTOU
Art editor: EVI DAMIRI
Photographs: Archive M. TOUBIS S.A., YIANNIS DESYPRIS

Production - Printing: M. TOUBIS S.A.